Ex-Library: Friends of
Lake County Public Library

AMERICA'S MOST WANTED

Public Enemy Number One:
JOHN H. DILLINGER

Written by:
Sue L. Hamilton

LAKE COUNTY PUBLIC LIBRARY

Published by Abdo & Daughters, 6537 Cecilia Circle, Bloomington, Minnesota 55435

Library bound edition distributed by Rockbottom Books, Pentagon Tower, P.O. Box 36036, Minneapolis, Minnesota 55435

Copyright© 1989 by Abdo Consulting Group, Inc., Pentagon Tower, P.O. Box 36036, Minneapolis, Minnesota 55435. International copyrights reserved in all countries. No part of this book may be reproduced in any form without written permission from the publisher. Printed in the United States.

Library of Congress Number: 89-084920   ISBN: 0-939179-60-1

Cover Photo by: Bettmann Archive
Inside Photos by: Bettmann Archive

3 3113 03279 0315

Edited by: John C. Hamilton

3

FORWARD

April 22, 1934

"Open fire!" screamed FBI Agent Melvin Purvis, the steely-eyed man in charge of the capture. The cold quiet surrounding the small resort in Rhinelander, Wisconsin was instantly shattered. Machine guns and pistols of dozens of G-men blasted in unison. Bullets shattered the doors and windows of the resort's main lodge. Inside hid American's Most Wanted, Public Enemy Number One: John Dillinger. "Keep firing and move in!" shouted Purvis.

The agents closed in. It was the moment of truth. The man who had robbed countless banks, terrified hundreds, and led an unstoppable crime wave was only a few feet away.

Purvis approached the lodge's door. "Cover me," he said. His Thompson submachine gun raised and ready, he lifted his foot and kicked. In an instant he'd know if the manhunt was a success . . .

With one swift motion he was inside, gun aimed, quickly eyeing every corner. Several agents rushed in behind him, guns ready. The only sound was the flutter of a curtain on an open window on the back cabin wall. Purvis glared across the cabin towards the open window. And then he heard a noise, the distant sound of a car engine starting. "Dillinger's escaped! Get the cars!"

Over a mile away from the trap set by Melvin Purvis, John Dillinger drove down one of many dark country roads. Headlights off, engine purring quietly, the stolen black car moved like a shadow in the night. Smiling, Dillinger said to his two companions, John "Three-Fingered Jack" Hamilton and Homer Van Meter, "They'll never find us on these back roads. This is the biggest screw-up the 'screws' ever pulled!"

"Yeah," said Van Meter, crouched in the back seat. "We made a clean getaway. The Feds never even checked the roof!"

"What's our next move, boss?" asked Hamilton, as Dillinger turned the car onto yet another back road.

"We're heading towards the Minnesota border, but I'm taking only the back roads," said Dillinger as he settled back into his seat. His reputation as a great escape artist still intact, the cool-headed gangster was already planning his next heist.

Miles back, gangbuster Melvin Purvis knew that this mission was his worst failure ever. He was already thinking of the report he'd have to make to his boss, J. Edgar Hoover, head of the FBI. The next couple days would be some of his worst. "There's no way we're going to find him out here," stated Purvis to the young FBI agent driving. "It's too dark, and we don't know the area like he does. Let's head back into town. We'll have the local police set up roadblocks across the state."

Turning the car around, the rookie muttered, "Dillinger made us look like fools. People depend on us to bring these gangsters to justice. How's it going to look?"

Staring straight ahead, Purvis responded quietly, "It's going to look like we have to start doing our job better than he's doing his. And that's exactly what I'm planning to do." Slamming his fist into his hand, Purvis' voice grew louder. "I'm taking Dillinger down," he promised. "That gangster is going to be in prison or dead by the end of this year. You can bet on that!"

CHAPTER 1 —
DILLINGER'S FIRST BIG MISTAKE

August 1924 — Ten Years Earlier. Martinsville, Indiana.

"You're a pretty fair shortstop," stated Edgar Singleton, the local baseball team's umpire.

"Thanks," said 21-year-old John Dillinger. "I'd like to play in the Big League. Maybe someday I'll get that chance."

"Money can help," said Singleton. "Look, see that man walking by . . ."

"You mean old Mr. Morgan? I've known him for years. Owns the grocery store down the road," said Dillinger.

"Yeah. Today's Friday. Tomorrow he'll be carrying home his whole week's earnings. He never packs a gun. It'd be easy pickings. We'll split it. Are you with me?" asked Singleton.

Dillinger hesitated. He already had a history of stealing (a couple cars and a few petty thefts). Plus he was AWOL, Away Without Leave, from the Navy. "I don't know about this . . ." he said to Singleton.

"Come on! It'd be easy. We don't have to hurt the guy. Besides, you'd have to work for a month to bring home half of what Morgan will have in his coat pocket tomorrow. You could take your share and head for Chicago. Maybe get in touch with a Minor League Baseball scout. What do you say? Are you in?"

Dillinger paused, thinking. "Yeah," he said. "I'm in."

Two weeks later . . .

"I turned myself in," said Dillinger to the Honorable Judge Joseph W. Williams, the toughest judge in the country. "Don't that count for nothin'?"

John Dillinger, notorious criminal in Indiana court. At right is Attorney Joesph Ryan.

"You are a criminal. A thief. You shot at and beat an unarmed man," said the judge, his eyes glaring down.

Dillinger swallowed. It didn't matter that he'd testified that Singleton was behind the whole thing. Singleton didn't turn himself in, and even after he was caught, he claimed he was innocent.

"You are a threat to the people of Indiana," stated Judge Williams, shuffling papers on his desk. "I believe in punishing crimes. You won't ever forget what you did two weeks ago! For your attack on Mr. Morgan, you will serve 2 to 14 years. For the attempted robbery, 10 to 20 years. Sentences are to be served one after the other. Now, get out of my sight!"

The court police grabbed Dillinger's arms. Ripping free, he turned back to Judge Williams. "You can put me away, Your Honor," said Dillinger in a voice icy cold. "But you can't keep me there! I'll get out and you and this whole country are going to be sorry!" With that, he turned and walked away.

CHAPTER 2 — THE GANG

"Ya got guts, I have to say that about you," said convicted bank robber Homer Van Meter, now playing catcher for the Pendleton Indiana Reformatory baseball team. "That was what, yer fourth try to escape?"

"Yup, fourth," said prisoner John Dillinger, swinging and hitting a long high ball that was lost in the sun by the outfielders. Home run!

Dillinger's time in prison had hardened him. He knew he could never be a professional baseball player, not with his record. It seemed the only thing left was to become a criminal. He knew he could be good at it . . . if he got the right training.

As the whistle blew ending their exercise time that summer morning of 1925, Dillinger met with Van Meter and the well-known and feared bank robber, Harry "Pete" Pierpont. Uncontrollable and violent, the two were being transferred to "the big house" in Michigan City: Indiana State Prison.

"Look, John," said Pierpont, "We haven't got much time. Here's the deal. You're smart. We've got experience. Find a way out of this joint, spring us outta' the big house, and we're in business."

"I'll find a way," said Dillinger, his mind already planning.

Dillinger never escaped from Pendleton. He tried to earn parole in 1929 by keeping out of trouble and gaining a reputation as an excellent baseball shortstop. However, the parole board was less than impressed with his record. He wasn't getting out early. More angry with the system than he had ever been before, Dillinger made one demand: "Transfer me to Indiana State Prison."

"What?! Why?" asked a confused parole board chairman. "Nobody *asks* to go to the big house!"

Thinking fast, Dillinger smiled and said, "They have a *real* baseball team up there."

On July 15, 1929, Dillinger stared up at the high, stark concrete wall surrounding Indiana's State Prison. As Inmate No. 13225, he walked with Van Meter and Pierpont, along with well-known bank robbers John "Three-Fingered Jack" Hamilton, Charles Makley, and Russell Clark.

"I have to learn everything I can about this place and about the business," stated Dillinger grimly. "I intend to spring you guys, and we're going to do some jobs so well that none of us will ever see the inside of a joint again."

"You've got a lot to learn, kid," said Pierpont. "Let's get started."

CHAPTER 3 —
THE GREAT ESCAPE

"OK, Dillinger, let's go," yelled the guard.

It was May 22, 1933. Dillinger's stepmother was dying. At the request of his father and nearly 200 people in his hometown (even Mr. Morgan!), he was released to rush to her bedside. She died an hour before he arrived.

Dillinger was saddened at her death, but it had earned him an early parole and he was free! He had spent nine years in prison learning everything he could about robbery. He had enough information stored in his brain to begin a crime wave. However, the first thing to do was spring his gang, and to do that, he needed money. Money to bribe guards. Money for guns, get-away cars, clothes, and a proper hideout.

Getting together a "gang" of small-time hoods, Dillinger pulled off some bank jobs. Most of them gained him less than $100, until September 6, 1933. Dillinger walked into The State Bank of Massachusetts Avenue in Indianapolis, pointed his gun at the bank's assistant manager, and said simply, "This is a stickup."

Dillinger walked out with the second-biggest heist in Indiana's history: $24,800. Hundreds of employees of the Real Silk Hosiery Company would go without paychecks for the month.

"How am I supposed to feed my family? Pay for my house?" asked one angry employee of the company. "I hope they catch him and string him up!"

"All my savings . . . gone," said an elderly lady with tears in her eyes. "What am I supposed to do, now? How will I live?"

None of this mattered to Dillinger. He had done what he set out to do. Now well funded with hundreds of innocent people's money, Dillinger put into action his plan to spring his gang still locked up in Indiana State Prison.

On September 19, Dillinger drove to Chicago, Illinois. Carrying four guns and several boxes of bullets wrapped in heavy paper, he entered a local warehouse. Slipping the foreman a $20 bill to look the other way, Dillinger opened a large box of thread that was being sent to the prison's shirt shop. Packing the guns and ammo under the spools of thread, he closed the box and marked it with a large red "X."

"That'll do it," said Dillinger with a smile. Next he drove his car to Dayton, Ohio. He had a couple days to wait and he was going to visit his girlfriend, Mary Longnaker. "It's up to the guys inside, now," he thought. But Dillinger's own luck didn't hold.

"He's upstairs," whispered landlady Lucille Stricker. Quietly, two detectives climbed the stairs to Miss Longnaker's room on the second floor.

"One, two, three . . ." whispered one of the detectives. Kicking in the door, the two rushed into the room, machine guns pointed directly at Dillinger. Mary Longnaker's scream echoed through the house.

16

"John Dillinger, you are under arrest for the suspected robbery of The State Bank of Massachusetts Avenue," barked the tall policeman, grabbing Dillinger up from his seat on the kitchen chair. "You're coming with us."

The following day, September 26, Pete Pierpont led nine of his fellow bank robbers on one of the greatest prison escapes of all time. Using the guns and ammo sent into the prison by Dillinger, Pierpont took several guards hostage and forced them to lead the group through the prison's security gates. Stealing two cars, the hoods made a clean get-away. Now locked away in an Ohio jail, Dillinger had master-minded the biggest jail break in the history of the country.

Never forgetting their friend, on October 12, Pierpont, Makley and Clark walked boldly into the jail house where Dillinger was being held. Facing Sheriff Jess Sarber, Pierpoint tried to convince the sheriff that they were officers from Indiana State Prison. "We want to talk to your prisoner," said Pierpont.

"Let's see some I.D." demanded Sheriff Sarber, looking at the three as if he knew something wasn't quite right.

"Here, will this do?!" asked Pierpont, whipping out a gun from behind his coat.

Before the sheriff could move, Pierpont had blasted two bullets into the big man, while the other two moved into the jail to release Dillinger.

Lying in a pool of blood, the sheriff caught Dillinger's eyes. Dillinger stopped for a moment, looking down at a man who had treated him well and whom he could help with one short phone call. He turned and walked out of the jail. The sheriff died that same night.

CHAPTER 4 —
AMERICA'S MOST WANTED

The gang was free. They were together. After all those years behind bars, now the "fun" started.

WANTED

JOHN HERBERT DILLINGER

On June 23, 1934, HOMER S. CUMMINGS, Attorney General of the United States, under the authority vested in him by an Act of Congress approved June 6, 1934, offered a reward of

$10,000.00

for the capture of John Herbert Dillinger or a reward of

$5,000.00

for information leading to the arrest of John Herbert Dillinger.

DESCRIPTION

Age, 32 years; Height, 5 feet 7-1/8 inches; Weight, 153 pounds; Build, medium; Hair, medium chestnut; Eyes, grey; Complexion, medium; Occupation, machinist; Marks and scars, 1/2 inch scar back left hand, scar middle upper lip, brown mole between eyebrows.

All claims to any of the aforesaid rewards and all questions and disputes that may arise as among claimants to the foregoing rewards shall be passed upon by the Attorney General and his decisions shall be final and conclusive. The right is reserved to divide and allocate portions of any of said rewards as between several claimants. No part of the aforesaid rewards shall be paid to any official or employee of the Department of Justice.

If you are in possession of any information concerning the whereabouts of John Herbert Dillinger, communicate immediately by telephone or telegraph collect to the nearest office of the Division of Investigation, United States Department of Justice. the local addresses of which are set forth on the reverse side of this notice.

JOHN EDGAR HOOVER, DIRECTOR,
DIVISION OF INVESTIGATION,
UNITED STATES DEPARTMENT OF JUSTICE,
WASHINGTON, D. C.

June 25, 1934

Dillinger master-minded each and every job. He learned everything he could about a bank. He timed everything. The jobs were done clean and quick. And, of course, there was always lots of money. From $74,728 in Indiana to $27,789 in Wisconsin, and back to Indiana for another $20,376. The police seemed unable to stop or even catch him.

Until . . .

On January 24, 1934, the police chief of Tucson, Arizona answered his phone. "Look," said a female voice on the other end of the line. "That Dillinger fella and his gang are staying at the hotel."

"Sure, sure," responded the chief, not paying much attention.

"It's him all right," said the voice. "I recognize him from his picture in the papers."

"OK, we'll send somebody to check it out," said the policeman and hung up.

The following day, Dillinger, Pierpont, Clark, and Makley were captured and arrested. As much as Dillinger loved all the stories published about him,

this time it had cost him. Immediately, he was sent to the "escape-proof" Crown Point Jail in Indiana to await trial.

March 3, 1934

"What ya got there?" asked Herbert Youngblood, a 35-year old murderer. "A gun?!"

"Yup," said Dillinger. "Cost me thousands to get it, but my lawyer had it smuggled in. I'm gettin' out — tonight!"

"I'm goin' too," said Youngblood.

Smiling, Dillinger raised his voice, "Guard! Guard!" The evening watchman approached the cell.

"I've got something for you!" said Dillinger, whipping out his pistol and pointing it directly in the face of the startled guard. "Open the door or die," he threatened. The guard unlocked the cell door, and Dillinger and Youngblood calmly walked out.

Heading for the warden's office, the two grabbed machine guns, and made their way past 50 deputies and National Guardsmen. Dillinger took two hostages. They escaped out a side door and into the prison garage. "We'll take the nice lady sheriff's car," laughed Dillinger, stepping into the driver's seat of Sheriff Lillian Holley's police car.

Dillinger drove away, free once again. Later, far away from any main roads, Dillinger let his two prisoners go unharmed. Youngblood also decided to go his own way. "Thanks for the ride," said the tall black man. "I owe ya one!"

This escape brought Dillinger national attention. However, the story that hit the papers told that Dillinger had carved a "wooden gun," blackened it with shoe polish, and tricked the police into believing it was real. No one questioned how this known criminal got a knife to carve the gun in the first place. After all, he was the man who could escape from anywhere. Dillinger loved the story. The police did not.

However, Dillinger had made one big mistake. He drove Sheriff Holley's car across the Indiana state line into Illinois. Taking a stolen vehicle across state lines is a *federal* offense. Now, among the clever titles the newspapers had given him, he could add one more courtesy of the FBI: "Public Enemy Number One."

CHAPTER 5 — HUNTED

Only three days after his escape, Dillinger entered a bank in Sioux Falls, South Dakota, and walked out with nearly $50,000. One week later, he made off with $52,000 from a Mason City, Iowa bank.

However, the police were hot on his tail. They were tired of his prank calls and letters. The newspapers were making him look like a super-crook, and making the police look like fools. Law officers across the country wanted Dillinger. And they wanted him badly.

Meantime, Dillinger, well supplied with other people's money, decided to lay low for awhile. In mid-April, together with his old prison pals John Hamilton and Homer Van Meter, and

"Baby Face" Nelson

accompanied by crazy-man "Baby Face" Nelson, he headed for the quiet resort of Little Bohemia in northern Wisconsin.

After a long drive across back-country roads, they finally arrived at the lodge. Although tired, Dillinger was no fool. "Homer," he said, "Map out the entire area, right now."

"Check," said Van Meter, turning back towards the car.

"The rest of you, let's scout this place out. I want to know how we can get out fast, if we have to."

On April 22, with their escape plans laid out, the criminals settled back to enjoy a quiet evening. The FBI, however, had other plans in mind. "Open fire!" screamed FBI Agent Melvin Purvis, the man in charge of the group of G-men who had tracked Dillinger to the resort.

At the first shot, Dillinger was up and headed for the window. "Come on!" he motioned to Van Meter and Hamilton. "Across the roof!"

With that, the three escaped, stealing a car from a nearby home. Nelson, in another cabin, also made his escape, but not before killing one FBI agent and wounding several others. However, once again, Dillinger, American's Most Wanted, had outsmarted the police.

CHAPTER 6 — THE LADY IN RED

"I can get him for you," said Detective Sgt. Martin Zarkovich of the East Chicago, Indiana Police Department.

"How?" asked Agent Melvin Purvis, leaning forward in his chair. Since that night in April, all he could think of was how to nab Dillinger.

"There's a foreign woman here in Chicago, see," continued Zarkovich. "She goes by the name Anna Sage. She shares a room with another woman, a Polly Hamilton. Polly is Dillinger's latest girlfriend. Now, here's the deal. Sage is about to be deported, sent back to where she came from, Rumania, I think. Anyway, if we can swing it so the U.S. Government lets her stay in America, she'll help us out."

Purvis didn't hesitate. "Set it up."

On the hot night of July 22, 1934, a well-watched trio walked toward Chicago's Biograph Theater, which advertised "Cooled By Refrigeration." "It'll be nice to get inside!" said Anna Sage nervously to John Dillinger and her friend Polly Hamilton. Dressed to be easily seen, Anna stepped in front of the theater lights. Her outfit glowed the color of blood red.

"There he is," said Purvis, sweat pouring down his face. "Too many people around to get him now," he said watching Dillinger walk inside the packed theater. "We'll have to wait until he comes out."

Two hours passed. Eyes aching, Purvis continued to stare at the theater doors. A little passed 10:30 p.m. the movie ended. Dillinger emerged with Polly holding one arm and Anna the other. Purvis lit his cigar, the signal the other agents were waiting for. They closed in. "I've finally got you!" thought Purvis, getting out of his car, ready to take Public Enemy Number One into custody.

Dillinger suddenly noticed both women had stopped several steps back from him. He looked around. "A trap! They led me into a trap," he thought, pulling a Colt automatic from his pants pocket and looking for an escape. Turning, he raced down the alley next to the theater.

Suddenly, several shots rang out. Startled, Purvis looked around. Detective Sgt. Martin Zarkovich had shot Dillinger as the criminal had turned to run. Amid frightened screams and confused yells, Zarkovich stood wordless, his gun still smoking.

Blood flowed freely from Dillinger's body as Melvin Purvis walked up. America's Most Wanted had been shot through the side and neck, dying instantly. "You couldn't escape this one, could you?" whispered Purvis to the dead criminal.

CHAPTER 7 — OR COULD HE?

Years later, facts led some investigators to believe that the man killed by the FBI was *not* John Dillinger, but James Lawrence, a small-time criminal who looked like the famous bank robber.

Dr. J. J. Kearns examined the body. His death report showed that the body taken from the Biograph Theater's alley had brown eyes

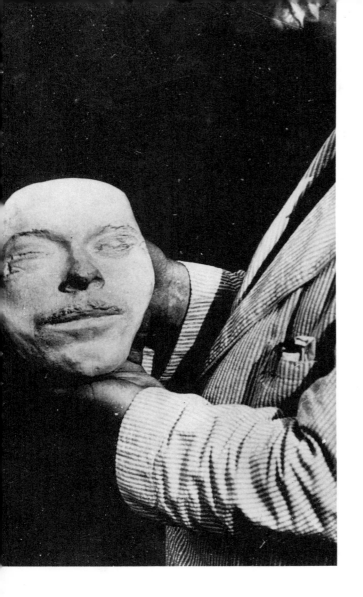 

(Dillinger's were blue), a heart condition (Dillinger had none), and was shorter and heavier than Dillinger. Also, the body had none of the scars or birthmarks that Dillinger bore. (Mysteriously, the doctor's report was lost or stolen. A copy of it was found some 30 years later.)

It is known that Dillinger had plastic surgery to alter his face and fingerprints. However, many believe James Lawrence was set up to die in place of John Dillinger, and that, in fact, Dillinger lived for years following his supposed "death." It is impossible to prove this theory, however, and to this day the FBI contends that it got the right man.

CHAPTER 8 —
WHAT ABOUT THE REST?

Edgar Singleton — The man who began Dillinger's road to crime back in 1924 got off with serving only two years in jail. In 1937, drunk, he fell asleep on some railroad tracks and was run over.

Harry "Pete" Pierpont — In September 1934, Pierpont tried and failed to escape from prison using Dillinger's "fake" gun idea (a pistol carved from soap). The following month he went to the electric chair.

Charles Makley — Killed while trying to escape with Pierpont.

Homer Van Meter — Double-crossed, he was gunned down by "friends" on August 23, 1934.

John "Three-Fingered Jack" Hamilton — Shot by a deputy sheriff several days after the gang's escape from the FBI in April 1934. Although Dillinger tried to get him to a doctor, Hamilton died.

Russell Clark — Spent most of his life behind bars. He was paroled in 1970 and died of cancer that same year.

Herbert Youngblood — On March 16, 1934, 13 days after escaping with Dillinger from Crown Point Prison, he was shot by three deputy sheriffs in the state of Michigan. Before dying, he lied to police claiming that Dillinger had been with him the day before. It was his way of paying his debt to Dillinger, because, of course, Dillinger was nowhere in the area.

"Baby Face" Nelson — Replacing Dillinger as Public Enemy Number One, Nelson killed two FBI agents in November 1934, dying himself shortly thereafter of wounds received in the battle.

Within a year and a half, the "Dillinger gang" was gone forever.